Ayobola's Success Equation
The mathematical formula to achieving success

$$S = (K / N) \times (O \times E \times R)$$

"Success is a calculated journey, where opportunity, effort, and resilience transform potential into reality."

By Dr Ayobola Adedayo

Introduction	3
Chapter 1- The Encounter	5
Chapter 2: The Catalyst	9
Chapter 3: The Application	11
Chapter 4: The Challenges	13
Chapter 5: The Journey Begins	15
Chapter 6: The Turning Point	17
Chapter 7: The Summit of Success	19
Chapter 8: The Legacy	21
Epilogue: The Journey Continues	23
How to utilise the success equation	25

Introduction

The pursuit of success can often feel like navigating a winding path with unforeseen twists and turns. We struggle with uncertainties, setbacks, and the fear of failure. But amidst these challenges

The Success equation, is a formula created to help fully grasp why luck can be improved upon with consistent efforts. This is a framework that helps to transcend the uncertainties of chance and charts a course towards achievement and fulfilment.

At its core, the Success equation embodies the principle that success is not merely a matter of luck as a standalone, but a strategic pursuit, which is a delicate balance of opportunity, effort, and resilience. It invites us to view success through a new lens that acknowledges the role of probability in shaping our destinies and empowers us to take control of our own narrative.

In the following chapters, we embark on a journey of exploration and discovery that is guided by the wisdom of the Success equation and the insights of those who have harnessed its power to achieve greatness.

Join me as we discuss the success equation, decode its fundamentals, and embark on a quest to unlock our full potential.

The journey ahead may be challenging, but with the guidance of the Success equation as our compass, we can navigate the complexities of life with confidence and clarity, knowing that the path to success lies within our grasp.paths to success. Along the way, we uncover the principles that lie at the heart of the Success equation and learn how to apply its principles to our own lives.

Chapter 1- The Encounter

In the heart of Lagos, Nigeria, Adebola Adeyemi was on her way to a business symposium. The symposium was filled with excitement as entrepreneurs and innovators from across the country gathered to exchange ideas and insights.

In the midst of the crowd, Ayobola Adedayo caught Adebola's attention with her air of authority and charisma. Ayobola was a renowned inventor and entrepreneur who had garnered widespread attention for her revolutionary theories on success.

Intrigued by Ayobola's presence, Adebola found herself drawn to the centre of the room where Ayobola was holding court with a group of eager listeners. As she listened intently to her words, Adebola felt a spark of curiosity ignite within her. She was keen to understand the secrets behind Ayobola's success.

Ayobola's teachings centred around a concept she called the Success equation(TSE). According to Ayobola, success was not a matter of luck, but a product of probabilities and persistence. She explained how the TSE could be used to analyse past failures and successes, identify patterns, and increase the likelihood of success in future endeavours.

Ayobola's voice resonated with authority as she detailed the components of the Success equation:

$$S = (K / N) \times (O \times E \times R)$$

"Success isn't a roll of the dice," Ayobola explained. "It's a numbers game. The more attempts you make (N), the greater your chances of success (S), provided you tackle the inherent difficulty or 'grind factor' (K) head-on."

Explanation of the Formula:

- S represents the overall success probability.
- N denotes the number of attempts made in pursuit of success.
- K signifies the inherent difficulty level or "grind factor" associated with the endeavour.
- O represents the opportunities present in a given situation, including factors such as market demand, timing, and competitive landscape.
- E reflects the level of effort, commitment, and dedication invested in the pursuit of goals.
- R signifies resilience—the ability to overcome setbacks, challenges, and obstacles encountered along the journey.

Example:

Let's consider an example to illustrate the Success equation:

Suppose an aspiring entrepreneur, Adebola, wants to launch a tech startup. She identifies a growing market demand (Opportunity, O = 0.8), but she also faces stiff competition and technical challenges (Difficulty, K = 0.6). Adebola is highly motivated and committed to her venture (Effort, E = 0.9), and she possesses a resilient mindset, willing to learn from failures and setbacks (Resilience, R = 0.7).

Now, let's plug these values into the formula:

S = (K / N) x (O x E x R)

S = (0.6 / 3) x (0.8 x 0.9 x 0.7)

S = (0.2) x (0.504) = 0.1008

In this scenario, Adebola's success probability (S) is approximately 10.08%. By understanding and optimising the factors influencing her success, such as increasing her number of attempts (N), refining her approach to tackle the inherent difficulty (K), and maximising opportunities (O), Adebola can enhance her chances of success in launching her tech startup.

Chapter 2: The Catalyst

Adebola left the symposium feeling excited, her mind consumed by Ayobola's powerful teachings on success. The Success equation resonated deeply with her, offering a new perspective on achieving her entrepreneurial dreams.

As she walked through the bustling streets of Lagos, Adebola felt that her encounter with Ayobola was more than a chance meeting, it was a catalyst for change. Inspired by Ayobola's Success equation, she decided to dive deeper into the principles of the Success equation and apply them to her life.

Back at her office, Adebola wasted no time researching, reading articles, books, and case studies related to the Success equation. With each new piece of information she uncovered, her understanding of the formula grew, and she began to see how it could be applied to her entrepreneurial endeavours.

One key insight that struck Adebola was the importance of resilience in the pursuit of success. As she read about entrepreneurs who overcame seemingly insurmountable obstacles, she realised that resilience was the fuel that powered their journey. With this knowledge, Adebola resolved to cultivate her resilience, knowing it would be crucial in navigating the challenges ahead.

Another aspect of the Success equation that resonated with Adebola was the concept of opportunity. She realised success was not just about luck - it was about recognizing and seizing opportunities when they presented themselves. With this in mind, Adebola began to approach her work with a renewed sense of purpose, constantly searching for new opportunities to grow and succeed.

As days turned into weeks, Adebola's understanding of the Success equation deepened, and she felt more confident in achieving her goals. With Ayobola's teachings as her guide, she knew no obstacle was too great, and no dream was beyond reach.

Little did Adebola know, her journey had only just begun. As she prepared to embark on the next chapter of her entrepreneurial adventure, she felt a sense of excitement and anticipation coursing through her veins. With the Success equation by her side, she knew the possibilities were endless, and she was ready to seize them.

Chapter 3: The Application

After gaining new knowledge and determination, Adebola put the principles of the Success equation into action for her entrepreneurial endeavours. She understood that success wasn't solely about having a great idea, but it was also about taking consistent action and persevering through challenges.

With this mindset, Adebola started to plan her next steps with meticulous detail. She identified potential market opportunities and created a comprehensive strategy to capitalise on them. She knew that success wouldn't come easily, but she was willing to work hard and stay on course.

As she executed her plan, Adebola encountered various obstacles and setbacks. Despite moments of doubt and frustration, she refused to let them deter her. She leaned on the Success equation's principles, increasing her efforts, staying resilient amid adversity, and seizing every chance that came her way.

Gradually, Adebola started to see progress. Her hard work and perseverance paid off as she achieved small victories and milestones. With each success, her confidence grew, fueling her determination to keep pushing forward.

However, success didn't come without its challenges. There were moments when Adebola felt overwhelmed and uncertain about the road ahead. During those times, she turned to the Success equation for guidance, reminding herself that success was a journey, not a destination, and that every setback was an opportunity to learn and grow.

As Adebola navigated the ups and downs of entrepreneurship, she remained committed to the Success equation's principles. She knew that success wasn't guaranteed, but by consistently and diligently applying the formula, she was increasing her chances of achieving her goals.

With every passing day, Adebola's confidence grew, and her vision for the future became clearer. She knew that the road ahead would be long and challenging, but she was prepared to face any obstacles that came her way. With the wisdom of the Success equation, she was determined to make her dreams a reality.

Chapter 4: The Challenges

As Adebola progressed on her entrepreneurial journey, she faced a series of challenges that tested her determination and resilience. These obstacles ranged from financial setbacks to unforeseen market shifts, and posed a real threat to her progress.

One of the biggest challenges that Adebola encountered was securing funding for her startup. Despite her best efforts to pitch her idea to investors and obtain financing, she was met with rejection after rejection. This was a discouraging blow that made it hard for her to maintain her confidence in the face of adversity.

However, Adebola refused to let these setbacks define her. Instead, she turned to the principles of the Success equation for guidance. She reminded herself that success was not about avoiding challenges but about overcoming them. With renewed determination, she redoubled her efforts to secure funding, exploring alternative avenues and thinking outside the box.

Another significant challenge that Adebola faced was navigating the competitive landscape of her industry. As she worked to establish her startup in a crowded market, she found herself facing stiff competition from larger, more established players. This was intimidating, but Adebola refused to be intimidated. Instead, she embraced the challenge and used it as motivation to innovate and differentiate herself from the competition.

Throughout her journey, Adebola encountered numerous other challenges, from technical setbacks to personal doubts and insecurities. However, with each obstacle, she grew stronger and more resilient. She knew that success was not about avoiding challenges, but about facing them head-on and learning from them along the way.

As she navigated the challenges of entrepreneurship, Adebola remained committed to the principles of the Success equation. She knew that success was not guaranteed, but by staying resilient, determined, and open to new opportunities, she was increasing her chances of achieving her goals.

With each challenge that she overcame, Adebola grew more confident in her ability to succeed. She knew that the road ahead would be difficult, but she was ready to face whatever obstacles came her way. Armed with the wisdom of the Success equation, she was determined to persevere and make her dreams a reality.

Chapter 5: The Journey Begins

As Adebola's journey unfolded, she realised that success was not simply a destination, but a transformative journey of growth and self-discovery. Through each setback and triumph, she learned valuable lessons about resilience, determination, and the pursuit of excellence.

Entrepreneurship presented Adebola with a unique opportunity for self-discovery. She embraced the uncertainty and ambiguity of the path ahead, knowing that it was all part of the process of becoming the person she was meant to be.

Throughout her journey, Adebola encountered a diverse array of experiences and opportunities that shaped her perspective and fueled her ambition. From networking events and industry conferences to late-night brainstorming sessions and moments of quiet reflection, she immersed herself fully in the entrepreneurial journey.

One of the defining moments of Adebola's journey came when a major setback occurred in her business. Despite her best efforts, a key partnership fell through, leaving her feeling defeated and uncertain about the future. It was a moment of reckoning for Adebola, and she was forced to confront her deepest fears and insecurities.

However, instead of giving in to despair, Adebola chose to view the setback as an opportunity for growth and renewal. She drew on the principles of the Success equation to guide her through the darkness, and with each passing day, she emerged stronger and more resilient, ready to tackle whatever challenges lay ahead.

As Adebola's journey continued, she found herself growing in ways she never thought possible. She discovered new strengths and capabilities within herself and forged meaningful connections with fellow entrepreneurs who shared her passion and drive.

But perhaps most importantly, Adebola discovered the true meaning of success. It wasn't about fame or fortune, but about the journey itself and the person she became along the way. With each step forward, she felt a sense of purpose and fulfilment that transcended any material reward.

As the journey unfolded, Adebola knew that she was just getting started. With the Success equation as her guide, she was ready to embrace whatever challenges and opportunities lay ahead, knowing that the journey itself was the greatest reward of all.

———

Chapter 6: The Turning Point

Adebola found herself at a critical juncture that would shape the trajectory of her journey. It was a moment of decision where the choices she made would have far-reaching implications for her future.

Standing at the edge of change, Adebola felt a surge of conflicting emotions - fear, uncertainty, excitement, and hope. She knew that the decision she was about to make would require courage and conviction, but it was necessary for her growth and development as an entrepreneur.

With the principles of the Success equation as her guiding light, Adebola weighed her options carefully. She considered the potential risks and rewards of each path, knowing that success was not guaranteed. But she also knew that by embracing uncertainty and taking calculated risks, she could increase her chances of achieving her goals.

In the end, Adebola chose to trust her instincts and follow her heart. She made the decision to pivot her business in a new direction, seizing upon an emerging opportunity that aligned with her values and vision for the future.

It was a bold move, fraught with uncertainty and risk, but Adebola knew that it was the right decision for her. With a sense of clarity and purpose, she forged ahead, ready to embrace the challenges and opportunities that lay ahead.

As she embarked on this new chapter of her journey, Adebola felt a renewed sense of energy and excitement. She knew that the road ahead would be difficult, but she was confident in her ability to navigate it with grace and resilience.

Armed with the wisdom of the Success equation and the courage to pursue her dreams, Adebola set out to conquer new frontiers and make her mark on the world. The turning point had arrived, and she was ready to seize the moment and write the next chapter of her story.

Chapter 7: The Summit of Success

After months of hard work, perseverance, and unwavering determination, Adebola found herself standing at the summit of success - a culmination of her efforts and sacrifices, and a testament to her resilience and tenacity.

The journey to this point had been long and arduous, filled with challenges and obstacles that tested her resolve and pushed her to her limits. But through it all, Adebola remained committed to her goals, never losing sight of the vision that had driven her forward.

As she looked out at the future before her, Adebola felt a profound sense of accomplishment wash over her. She had overcome adversity, defied the odds, and achieved what many had thought impossible. But more than that, she had proven to herself that she was capable of greatness - that she had what it took to succeed in the face of adversity.

But as Adebola basked in the glow of her success, she knew that the journey was far from over. Success was not a destination, but a journey , it is a continuous process of growth, learning, and evolution. And as she looked toward the horizon, she saw endless possibilities stretching out before her, waiting to be explored.

With the principles of the Success equation as her guide, Adebola knew that she was ready to take on whatever challenges lay ahead. She had learned valuable lessons along the way such as resilience, determination, and the power of perseverance and she was stronger and more prepared than ever to face the future.

As she stood at the summit of success, Adebola made a silent vow to herself to never stop striving, never stop pushing the boundaries of what was possible, and never stop chasing her dreams. The journey had been long and difficult, but it had been worth every moment. And as she looked ahead to the next chapter of her life, Adebola knew that the best was yet to come.

Chapter 8: The Legacy

As Adebola's journey was nearing its end, she pondered on the legacy she would like to leave behind. She wished to be remembered for inspiring, empowering, and creating possibilities for others. Adebola believed that success was not only about personal achievements but also about positively impacting the world and leaving behind a lasting legacy for future generations.

Adebola had achieved more than she ever thought possible, all thanks to the Success equation that was her guiding light. However, she knew that her journey was not hers alone but one that would inspire others to pursue their own dreams and realise their full potential.

Throughout her journey, Adebola encountered numerous individuals who inspired and supported her. Her network of mentors, advisors, friends, and family had been a blessing, helping her navigate the challenges of entrepreneurship, and emerge stronger on the other side.

Reflecting on her journey, Adebola felt grateful and humbled. She knew that she had been fortunate to have had the opportunities and resources that had enabled her to succeed. She was determined to pay it forward by helping others achieve their dreams.

Adebola promised to use her influence and platform to support aspiring entrepreneurs and changemakers, whether through mentorship, advocacy, or philanthropy. She vowed to do everything possible to create opportunities for others to succeed and thrive.

Looking towards the future, Adebola felt optimistic and excited about the possibilities that lay ahead. With the Success equation as her legacy, she knew that she had the power to make a difference in the world and leave a lasting impact for generations to come.

As Adebola's journey came to an end, she felt a deep sense of satisfaction knowing that she had lived a life of purpose and meaning. With her legacy secure, she stepped boldly into the next chapter of her life, ready to embrace whatever challenges and opportunities lay ahead with courage, determination, and unwavering optimism.

Epilogue: The Journey Continues

As Adebola's story came to an end, a new chapter began, filled with infinite possibilities and untapped potential. With the guidance of the Success equation, Adebola embarked on the next phase of her journey with courage, determination, and unwavering optimism.

Equipped with the knowledge and wisdom gained from her experiences, Adebola felt a renewed sense of purpose and direction. Although she knew that the road ahead would not be easy, she was confident in her ability to overcome any obstacles that might come her way.

As she gazed towards the horizon, Adebola felt a sense of excitement and anticipation for what the future held. With the Success equation as her compass, she knew that the possibilities were endless and that she had the power to shape her destiny.

So, with a heart full of hope and a spirit full of determination, Adebola embarked on her next great adventure. With each step forward, she felt a sense of joy and fulfilment, knowing that she was living her life with purpose and intention.

As the journey continued, Adebola knew that there would be challenges and setbacks along the way. But she also knew that with the Success equation as her guide, she had everything she needed to succeed.

Thus, with a smile on her face and a fire in her heart, Adebola stepped boldly into the unknown, ready to embrace whatever the future had in store. For her, the journey was just beginning, and she couldn't wait to see where it would take her.

How to utilise the success equation

1. **Define Your Goals:** Clearly define your short-term and long-term goals across different aspects of your life, such as career, personal development, health, and relationships.

2. **Identify Opportunities (O)**: Conduct thorough research to identify opportunities aligned with your goals. This may include market demand for a business venture, job openings in your desired field, or avenues for personal growth and fulfilment.

3. **Commit Effort (E):** Develop a plan of action for each goal, outlining the specific steps you need to take to achieve them. Allocate dedicated time and resources to execute these plans consistently.

4. **Build Resilience (R):** Cultivate a resilient mindset to navigate challenges and setbacks. Practice self-care, stress management, and positive self-talk to maintain your mental and emotional well-being during difficult times.

5. **Address Difficulty (K):** Identify potential barriers or challenges that may hinder your progress towards your goals. Break down these challenges into smaller, actionable tasks and develop strategies to overcome them.

6. **Take Action:** Implement your plans with determination and persistence. Stay focused on your objectives, and be proactive in seizing opportunities and addressing obstacles as they arise.

7. **Monitor and Adjust:** Regularly assess your progress towards your goals using the Success Equation framework. Reflect on what's working well and where improvements can be made. Adjust your strategies and actions accordingly to stay on track towards success.

8. **Celebrate Milestones:** Celebrate your achievements and milestones along the way, no matter how small. Acknowledge your progress and use it as motivation to keep moving forward towards your ultimate objectives.

This framework provides clear distinctions between different levels of performance based on the overall percentage score.

You can use this table to track your progress, make adjustments, and continuously improve your chances of success by iteratively refining your values and strategies based on your evolving circumstances and objectives.

Component	Weightage	Explanation	Score (1-10)	Weighted Score

N	20%	Number of attempts made in pursuit of success		
K	20%	Inherent difficulty or "grind factor" of the endeavour		
O	20%	Opportunities present in a given situation		
E	20%	Level of effort, commitment, and dedication invested		
R	20%	Resilience—the ability to overcome setbacks and challenges		

In this framework:

- Enter values between 1 to 10 for each component based on your assessment of their significance to your goals.
- Assign weights to each component based on their relative importance in achieving success.
- Calculate the overall success probability (S) using the Success Equation formula, taking into account the values and weights assigned to each component.

Scoring breakdown

- 90% - 100%: A+
- 80% - 89%: A

- 70% – 79%: B+
- 60% – 69%: B
- 50% – 59%: C
- Below 50%: Fail

Let's calculate a sample score:

Component	Weightage	Explanation	Score (1-10)	Weighted Score
N	20%	Number of attempts made in pursuit of success	7	1.4
K	20%	Inherent difficulty or "grind factor" of the endeavour	8	1.6
O	20%	Opportunities present in a given situation	6	1.2

E	20%	Level of effort, commitment, and dedication invested	9	1.8
R	20%	Resilience—the ability to overcome setbacks and challenges	7	1.4

Now, let's calculate the weighted score for each component:

- Weighted Score for N = (20% of 7) = 0.20 * 7 = 1.4
- Weighted Score for K = (20% of 8) = 0.20 * 8 = 1.6
- Weighted Score for O = (20% of 6) = 0.20 * 6 = 1.2
- Weighted Score for E = (20% of 9) = 0.20 * 9 = 1.8
- Weighted Score for R = (20% of 7) = 0.20 * 7 = 1.4

Now, let's sum up the weighted scores:

Total Weighted Score = 1.4 + 1.6 + 1.2 + 1.8 + 1.4 = 7.4

Finally, let's calculate the overall percentage:

Overall Percentage = (Total Weighted Score / Total Weightage) * 100 = (7.4 / 10) * 100 = 74%

So, in this example, the overall percentage score is 74%, indicating a strong performance across all components.

- 90% - 100%: A+
- 80% - 89%: A
- 70% - 79%: B+
- 60% - 69%: B
- 50% - 59%: C
- Below 50%: D

Component	Actionable Recommendations
K (Difficulty)	<ul><li>Break down large tasks into smaller, manageable steps</li><li>Develop specific skills or acquire necessary knowledge to overcome challenges</li><li>Seek mentorship or guidance from experts in the field</li><li>Embrace failure as a learning opportunity and persist in the face of setbacks</li><li>Utilise tools or resources to streamline processes and reduce complexity</li><li>Prioritise tasks based on urgency and importance to minimise overwhelm</li></ul>

N (Number of Attempts)	<ul><li>Set clear, achievable goals to increase motivation and focus</li><li>Break goals into smaller tasks for easier management and progress tracking</li><li>Establish a routine or schedule for regular practice and iteration</li><li>Seek feedback and learn from failures to refine future attempts</li><li>Embrace a growth mindset, viewing challenges as opportunities for growth</li><li>Utilise resources and support networks to stay motivated and accountable</li></ul>
O (Opportunities)	<ul><li>Actively seek out new opportunities for growth and advancement</li><li>Expand professional networks through networking events or online platforms</li><li>Stay informed about industry trends and market developments</li><li>Be open to new experiences and willing to take calculated risks</li></ul>

	- Cultivate a reputation for reliability, professionalism, and excellence
- Leverage personal strengths and unique skills to capitalise on opportunities
E (Effort)	- Set ambitious yet realistic goals to challenge and motivate yourself
- Develop a strategic plan with actionable steps to achieve your objectives
- Prioritise tasks and manage time effectively to maximise productivity
- Cultivate a strong work ethic and commitment to excellence
- Continuously seek ways to improve and optimise your performance
- Stay disciplined and focused on your goals, even when faced with distractions
R (Resilience)	- Cultivate a positive mindset and outlook, focusing on solutions rather than problems
- Practice self-care and stress management techniques to build emotional resilience

	<ul><li>Surround yourself with supportive and encouraging individuals who uplift and inspire you</li><li>Develop coping strategies to deal with adversity and setbacks</li><li>Learn from past failures and setbacks, using them as stepping stones to future success</li><li>Stay adaptable and flexible in the face of change, embracing new opportunities for growth</li></ul>

www.ingramcontent.com/pod-product-compliance
Lightning Source LLC
Chambersburg PA
CBHW050254230526
45470CB00005B/2257